GOVINDA DIVYA CHARITAM VOLUME I

THE DIVINE STORIES OF GOVINDA

V RAMA KRISHNA

AF487757

Copyright © V Rama Krishna
All Rights Reserved.

This book has been self-published with all reasonable efforts taken to make the material error-free by the author. No part of this book shall be used, reproduced in any manner whatsoever without written permission from the author, except in the case of brief quotations embodied in critical articles and reviews.

The Author of this book is solely responsible and liable for its content including but not limited to the views, representations, descriptions, statements, information, opinions and references ["Content"]. The Content of this book shall not constitute or be construed or deemed to reflect the opinion or expression of the Publisher or Editor. Neither the Publisher nor Editor endorse or approve the Content of this book or guarantee the reliability, accuracy or completeness of the Content published herein and do not make any representations or warranties of any kind, express or implied, including but not limited to the implied warranties of merchantability, fitness for a particular purpose. The Publisher and Editor shall not be liable whatsoever for any errors, omissions, whether such errors or omissions result from negligence, accident, or any other cause or claims for loss or damages of any kind, including without limitation, indirect or consequential loss or damage arising out of use, inability to use, or about the reliability, accuracy or sufficiency of the information contained in this book.

Made with ♥ on the Notion Press Platform
www.notionpress.com

Dedicated to

To those who believe, and to those who are searching

-may these stories bring you closer to Govinda

Contents

Foreword

This book is a small offering of love and devotion to Govinda, the one who listens to our prayers and walks with us every step of the way.

The stories in these pages are filled with faith, miracles, and the presence of Lord Venkateswara. Some are based on real experiences, some inspired by divine legends — but all of them carry one message: Govinda is always with us, even when we don't see Him.

I wrote this book with the hope that it will touch your heart, give you hope, and bring you closer to the divine. Whether you are young or old, reading for the first time or the hundredth, may these stories bring peace and faith into your life.

In service to Govinda,

Rama Krishna

Preface

In our busy lives, it's easy to forget that the divine is always with us. Lord Venkateswara, also known as Govinda, has been a source of peace and strength for millions. His miracles and blessings are beyond our understanding, yet they touch our hearts and guide us through difficult times.

This book brings together stories inspired by Govinda, filled with faith, love, and devotion. Some are ancient legends, while others are real-life experiences — all meant to remind us that the divine is always near, watching over us, and ready to help when we call out.

Whether you've known Govinda for years or are just beginning to learn about Him, may these stories bring you closer to the divine and fill your heart with peace and hope.

May these stories help you feel the light and love of Govinda in your life
-Rama Krishna

ACKNOWLEDGEMENTS

I offer my heartfelt gratitude to Sri Venkateswara Swamy (Govinda) for His blessings and guidance. Without His presence in my life, this book would not have been possible.

I also thank everyone who has supported and encouraged me through my journey on Instagram. Your trust and inspiration have meant so much.

With sincere gratitude,
Rama Krishna
Instagram: @krishv_rama

PROLOGUE

In our lives, there are times when we feel uncertain, lost, or in need of guidance. During these moments, many of us turn to faith and seek help from something greater than ourselves. Sri Venkateswara Swamy, also known as Govinda, has been a source of hope, strength, and peace for countless people.

The stories shared in this book come from real experiences shared by people on my Instagram page. While these experiences are deeply personal, the identities of those who shared them have been kept private to respect their privacy. These stories reflect the love, miracles, and presence of Govinda in their lives.

As you read through these pages, I hope you feel the same comfort and inspiration that these real-life stories bring. They remind us that Govinda is always by our side, offering His guidance and care.

May Govinda's blessings bring peace to your heart, and may these stories inspire you to trust in His presence and love.

I

One Last Walk With Amma

Devotee is From Bangalore

Krishna had finally made it. After years of darkness, failures, and rejections, he had built a successful career in Hyderabad. From being mocked by relatives to owning his own company, life had turned—but one person never once doubted him: his Amma.

She had stood by him when even his own shadow seemed to avoid him. Krishna was planning something grand for her birthday.

But one evening, after dinner, she looked at him and gently said,

"My birthday is coming, kanna... Shall we go to Tirumala on foot this year? Maybe we can leave all these issues behind."

'My birthday is coming, kanna...
Shall we go to Tirumala on
foot this year?'

The Walk Begins

Krishna was surprised. Amma never asked for anything. But he agreed. He cancelled meetings, paused his business, and began the Tirumala padayatra with her.

She never told him the truth—that she had cancer. She smiled, walked, prayed... and quietly carried her pain, because she didn't want to burden her son again, not after watching him rise from the ashes.

Lessons on the Way

Each night during the yatra, Amma spoke words that stayed with Krishna forever."Govinda listens, kanna... not to our complaints, but to our silence."She taught him about trust, forgiveness, detachment, and faith.

"Life doesn't get easier, Krishna... we just become softer inside, and stronger outside."Her words were like medicine for wounds Krishna never spoke of.

The Divine Hill

At the foot of Alipiri, Amma touched the steps and whispered,
"Each one is a tear, kanna... we'll leave them all behind."
As they climbed, Krishna noticed her stopping often, her breathing slower. But she never complained. She just smiled every time she said "Govinda."
He didn't realize... this would be her last climb

The Final Birthday

They reached the temple. The darshan was magical. The crowd parted, the moment stood still. Amma folded her hands and looked at the Swamy for a long, long time.Back home, Krishna celebrated her birthday with her favorite sweets. She smiled and said,
    "I already got my gift... I saw Govinda, with you beside me."

The Truth After Goodbye

Weeks later, Amma collapsed. That's when Krishna found out—Stage 4 cancer.

She had known it. She had hidden it.

After her funeral, Krishna found a sealed envelope inside her wardrobe, tucked with a small photo of Venkateswara Swamy.

It read:

"My dear Krishna,

I never told you… because I didn't want to bring sorrow back into your life. You had just begun to live. I wanted one last walk… with my son, to my Govinda.

Because I know, once I'm gone, He will take care of you. He always has. He always will.

I love Him like I love you—silently, completely, forever.

Don't cry, kanna. I am still walking behind you. And Govinda… He's still ahead.

With all my love,

Amma.

A Life Rewritten

Krishna wept for days. Not just in grief—but in gratitude. He promised to help cancer patients as much as he could. Every year, on her birthday, Krishna walks the same path barefoot, with her letter in his shirt pocket.

And every time he sees Swamy, he hears Amma's voice:

"He's still ahead. Walk on, Krishna… walk on."

II
Where Tears met Govinda

Devotee is From Pune

A Mother's Pride – Tirupati Railway Station

Padma, a mother from a small village, stood at the station with her 25-year-old son, Varun. He had just received a job offer abroad — a dream he and Padma had prayed for years. Before leaving the country, he said, "Amma, let's visit Tirumala. I want to thank Govinda for everything." With tears of pride in her eyes, she replied, "Let's go, nanna. What more can a mother ask?" They boarded a private car, hearts filled with gratitude.

The Tragedy – Near Alipiri

As the Tirumala hills peeked through the morning mist, the car climbed the ghat road. Padma was singing Govinda Namalu. Suddenly—a loud honk. A lorry lost control on the curve. A sharp turn. A devastating crash.

The world went black.

When Padma opened her eyes, she was on the ground, blood on her forehead, and her son lay silent, covered in broken glass. "VARUN!!" she screamed. He didn't move. Ambulance sirens echoed.

The ICU – A Mother's Worst Fear

Doctors said, "Massive trauma. Very slim chance. He may not make it through the night."

Padma watched her son's body filled with tubes. His face was pale, lifeless.

She didn't argue. She didn't shout. She stepped out.

With bleeding feet, no slippers, and one old folded letter to Govinda, she started walking—toward Alipiri steps, alone, in the dead of night.

The Yatra – Amma's Plea

Padma began climbing the 3,550 steps, every step a cry, every breath a prayer.

At Mokali Parvatham, her legs collapsed. Her knees hit the stone. She trembled, holding the letter to her heart.

"Govinda... I carried him in my womb, I raised him with nothing... I can live with pain, hunger, and death... but not without his smile. Please... do this one miracle for a mother."

She placed the letter under a small stone and whispered, "This is not a request. This is a mother's soul I'm giving you."

The Divine Darshan

By dawn, she reached Tirumala temple. Her saree was torn, feet blistered, face swollen from crying.

She left her phone in the locker, washed her face, and entered the queue.

When the doors of the sanctum opened and Sri Venkateswara Swamy stood before her, she collapsed to her knees.

She didn't speak. She just folded her hands, looked up with tears streaming, and let her silence cry out.

"Govinda... I surrender."

The Bell Rings Twice

As she stepped out of darshan, the temple bells rang—once... twice.

She touched her heart and felt a strange warmth. Something had changed.

Moments later, in the temple cloakroom, she checked her phone.

12 missed calls.

Her fingers shook as she called back.

The Miracle

The nurse on the other end said, "Amma! He opened his eyes just as the sun rose! He said your name. He's alive. Breathing on his own now!"

Padma dropped the phone, fell to the floor outside the temple, and sobbed. Not in pain... but in surrender.

(There is no end to Your grace and love, Govinda.)

The Letter Was Gone

A week later, Padma returned to Mokali Parvatham. She searched for the stone. The place where she had placed the letter.

The stone was there.

The letter was gone.

In its place... a fresh tulasi leaf.

She smiled through tears. No words. Just silence.

Because now, she knew —

"A mother's cry reaches Him... even before it's spoken."

III

Govinda Stands for us

Devotee is From Rajahmundry

A simple middle-class family had waited for this divine yatra for nearly a year. Not for a holiday... not for a function... but for one sacred purpose — to have *darshan of Govinda.*

The father, Srinivas, ran a small electrical repair shop in a small town. Life was tough — daily struggles with money, school fees, and family needs. But one promise stayed in his heart. He had told his aged mother, "Amma, I'll take you to Tirumala. You must see Him once before your health fades. That is my word."

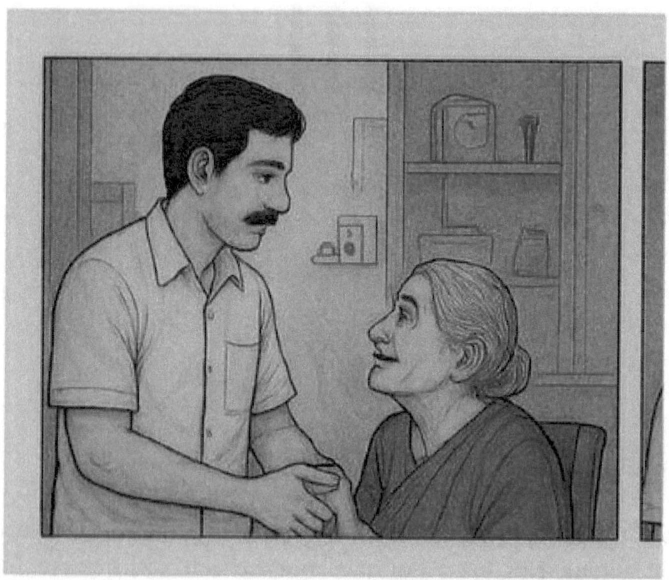

Devotion Over Pain

His mother, now weak and unable to walk properly, had only one wish left in her heart — to see the Lord one last time. Her knees hurt, her body was tired, but her devotion was full of strength.

Srinivas, his wife Lakshmi, their 9-year-old son Raju, and his mother started their holy journey to the sacred hills of Tirumala. Before sunrise, they joined the long darshan queue. The hours felt endless. People leaned on railings, some sat on the floor, some cried in pain — but the old mother softly chanted, "Govinda... Govinda..."

Innocent Question and A Mother's Answer

At one point, little Raju asked, "Amma, why doesn't God sit down? Won't He feel tired?"

Lakshmi gently replied, "Swamy stands for us, kanna. He doesn't sit, because He is still listening to everyone's prayers. Even when we sleep, He remains awake."

Darshan that Heals

Finally, they reached the sanctum. The moment they saw Lord Venkateswara, everything stopped. The heat, the pain, the tiredness — all forgotten.

Srinivas folded his hands with tears. The old mother cried silently. Raju looked at Swamy without blinking. In that one moment, they didn't see a statue — they saw a Living God, standing with strength and love, carrying everyone's burdens without a word.

That night, when the crowd was gone and the temple became silent, the senior priest came for *Ekantha Seva* — the Lord's resting time.

Words from a Priest's Heart

He folded his hands, looked at Swamy, and whispered with emotion:
   "Swamy... You've been standing since early morning.
   Lakhs of people came to see You...
   But You didn't move, You didn't rest.
   Even Ekantha Seva is short now...
   Before You even close Your eyes, Suprabhata begins again.
   You never sleep...
   Because You love us too much to rest."

• 19 •

Govinda's Voice

That night, little Raju had a dream.

He saw Swamy standing alone in the sanctum. Behind Him were piles of people's pain, prayers, and hopes. And yet, Swamy was calm, peaceful... still standing.

Raju heard a soft divine voice:

"Tell your ammamma(Grand mother)... I held her hand in the queue.

Tell your father... I saw every tear he didn't show.

Tell the world...

I stand without sleep.

Because their faith keeps Me awake.

I am their strength. I am their hope. I am their Govinda."

The Sleepless God

**He is the Sleepless God.

Not because He is tired...

But because His *love never rests.***

Even when the temple doors close,

He watches.

Even when darshans end,

He listens.

Even when we forget Him,

He remembers us — while still standing... for us.

IV
The Lost Faith

<u>*Devotee is From Hyderabad*</u>

When Faith is Lost... and Found again

Varun was a young software engineer working in Hyderabad. A self-made man, he had risen from a humble background to achieve success in life. But in the race to earn money, he had slowly drifted away from his faith. His mother, a devoted believer of Sri Venkateswara Swamy, would often ask him to visit Tirumala with her, but he always made excuses.

"Amma, all these rituals are outdated. God doesn't need me to stand in long queues or break coconuts," he would say.

The call that changed Everything

One day, Varun received an urgent call from his father. His mother had collapsed at home. By the time he rushed to the hospital, the doctors informed him that she had suffered a brain hemorrhage and was in a coma. His world shattered in an instant. The same mother whom he had always found strong and energetic now lay lifeless before him. The doctors gave no hope. "Prepare for the worst," they said.

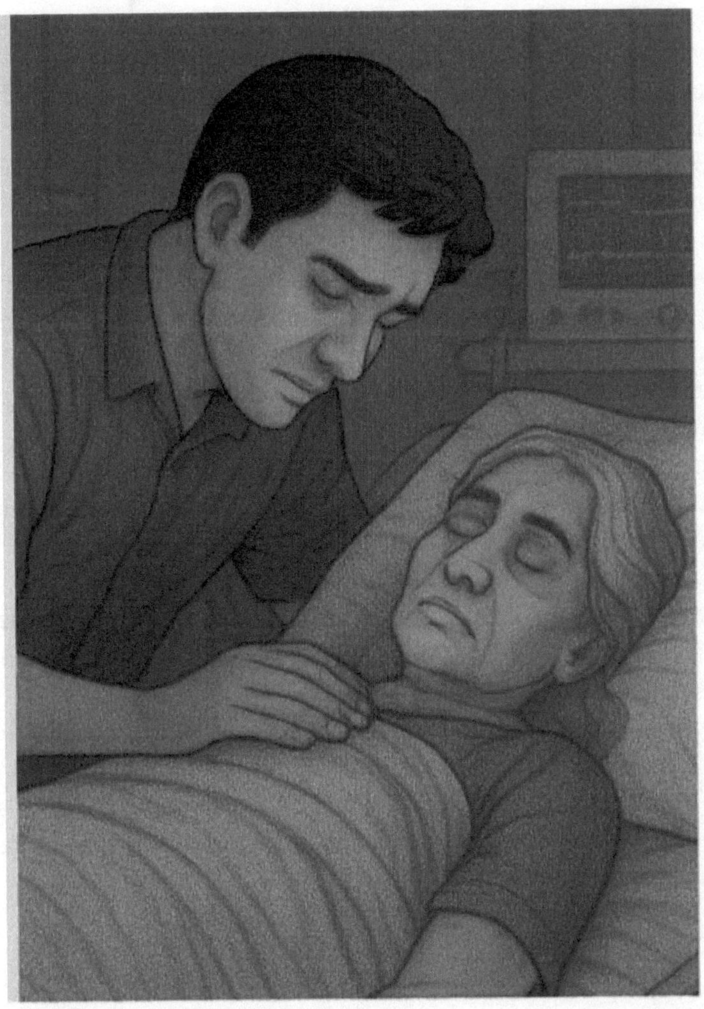

A Forgotten Message, A Desperate Prayer

Varun sat beside her bed, tears streaming down his face. He felt helpless. That night, as he scrolled through his phone, a message popped up in an old WhatsApp group—"Miracles of Lord Venkateswara." He opened it absentmindedly, only to see a post his mother had once sent:

"Even when we forget Him, Sri Venkateswara Swamy never forgets us. Call upon Him with true devotion, and He will answer in ways beyond our understanding."

Something inside him broke. He felt guilty for ignoring his mother's faith, for dismissing something that had given her strength all these years. Desperate, he whispered, "Swamy, if You are truly there, bring my Amma back. I will come to Your temple barefoot."

That night, he dreamt of Tirumala. He saw a golden light, and in it, a tall, majestic figure with a shankha and chakra. A deep voice echoed, "Your mother's time has not come. But remember, faith is not just for moments of despair. Keep it alive always."

Varun woke up in shock, his heart pounding. Just then, the doctor ran into the ICU. "Something unbelievable has happened! She is responding!"

Tears of joy and disbelief filled Varun's eyes. Within days, his mother miraculously recovered, defying all medical expectations. The first thing she said when she gained consciousness was, "Did you pray, Varun?" He held her hand tightly and whispered, "Yes, Amma. And He answered."

The Walk That Healed a Soul

True to his promise, Varun walked barefoot to Tirumala. As he stood before Sri Venkateswara Swamy, tears streamed down his face. He wasn't just here for his mother—he had found his lost faith.

V
The Devotee Who Was Never Alone

Devotee is From Small Streets of Samalkota

The Forgotten Devotee

In a small village, there stood a humble temple of Sri Venkateswara Swamy at its center. It was not grand or famous, just a simple temple where a small oil lamp flickered every day, kept alive by an elderly woman named Varalakshmi.

Despite her old age and fragile health, Varalakshmi dedicated her life to the temple. With the little government pension she received, she ensured that the temple remained active. She would light the lamps, offer harathi, and on every Ekadasi, she performed special pujas. Whatever little she could afford, she would distribute as prasadam—sometimes roasted chickpeas, sometimes whatever she had left.

There were days when she had no money at all, when she had to sleep on an empty stomach. Yet, she never let her devotion waver.

The villagers often questioned her, "At your age, why waste your money on the temple? You could use it for yourself." But while many had opinions, no one stepped forward to help. They only watched, criticizing her choices but never offering assistance.

The Lonely Departure

One day, tragedy struck—Varalakshmi suffered a heart attack and passed away alone in her small hut near the temple. Since she had no family, no one noticed her absence for a long time.

It was only when the villagers saw that the temple lamp had not been lit for the first time in years that they grew concerned. When they went to check on her, they found her lifeless body lying on the floor. A single photograph of Sri Venkateswara Swamy rested on her chest. Her frail hands still clutched a dried-up tulsi leaf, as if she had been offering it to the Lord even in her final moments.

The villagers hesitated over what to do. Conducting her final rites required money, and no one was willing to take responsibility. "She had no family, no children... why spend money on her?" they murmured among themselves. Finally, they decided to inform the municipal authorities, who agreed to take her body in the evening for disposal—treating her like an orphaned soul.

As the sun set, the villagers dispersed, leaving her alone once more.

The Divine Intervention

Just then, a physically disabled man named Raghav arrived. He was a poor villager who survived on a small government pension, much like Varalakshmi. When he heard what had happened, he rushed to her hut.

Seeing her lifeless form, he felt a lump in his throat. "She gave everything for Swamy... and now, she is abandoned like this?" His hands trembled as he turned to the villagers and said, "I will conduct her final rites with my own pension."

The villagers were shocked. "Why waste your money on this?" they asked. "You need it for yourself."

But Raghav remained firm. "This is not about money. Performing her final rites is a divine command for me. I do not need anyone's approval."

With great difficulty due to his disability, he arranged for a simple pyre. He placed her body gently, whispering, "Amma... you lived for Swamy, and yet, no one stood by you in your final moments. But I won't let you leave like an orphan."

As he was about to light the fire, a sudden gust of wind blew, and the temple bells rang loudly, even though the temple was empty. The villagers, hearing the bells ring at such an odd hour, rushed back, sensing something unusual.

To their shock, they saw Varalakshmi's body covered in a mysterious golden glow. The garland from Sri Venkateswara Swamy's idol had somehow fallen from the deity and was now resting on her chest. Raghav, with tears in his eyes, folded his hands.

"Swamy Himself has come for His devotee," he whispered.

At that very moment, the lamps inside the temple, which had remained unlit since Varalakshmi's passing, suddenly flickered to life on their own. A divine fragrance spread through the air. The villagers who once ignored her now fell to their knees, trembling in realization.

One of the elderly men in the village, his voice shaking, said, "We spent our lives running behind wealth and comfort, while she spent every penny for Swamy... and today, He has come for her. We failed to recognize a true devotee among us."

Tears streamed down Raghav's face. "Daivam ni sevinche vaadini manam opika lekunda choosam... kaani daivam maathram tana bhaktini vadiledu" ("We neglected the one who served God, but God never abandoned His devotee").

One by one, the villagers, ashamed of their ignorance, came forward. Those who had once refused to contribute now fell at Varalakshmi's feet, seeking forgiveness. But it was too late.

As the fine burned, the sky roared, and a light drizzle began—almost as if the heavens themselves were crying. Raghav watched the flames rise, whispering, "Amma... you are not alone. Swamy has taken you home."

That night, not a single soul in the village could sleep. The weight of their mistake hung over them like an unbearable burden. But for Raghav, there was only peace—because he knew the truth.

Varalakshmi was never abandoned. She had always been in the hands of Sri Venkateswara Swamy.

VI
Govinda Stands With Me

<u>*Devotee is From Hyderabad*</u>

The Temple Steps of Memories

Suneetha stood at the temple steps, the golden rays of the setting sun casting long shadows. She had once climbed these very steps with Arjun, her hands folded in prayer, believing that the love she held would last a lifetime. She had been a fool.

Now, she stood alone, her heart nothing but shattered pieces she no longer had the strength to gather.

The Day He Left

She still remembered the way Arjun had walked away from her. No guilt. No hesitation. Just cold detachment.

"It's over, Suneetha."

Those three words had ripped her soul apart.

She had begged. She had sobbed, clutching onto his shirt like a desperate child, pleading, "Don't do this. I gave you everything. I became everything you wanted me to be. Why, Arjun? Why?"

And then he had said it. The words that destroyed whatever little hope she had left.

"I never loved you the way you loved me."

When Prayers Go Silent

She had collapsed. Right there on the cold floor, gasping for breath, her chest burning with a pain she never knew was possible. He didn't even look back. Seven years, and he didn't even look back.

The days that followed were a blur of agony. She forgot how to eat, how to sleep. Every moment felt like suffocation, like the world was closing in on her. She prayed to Govinda every day, but He never answered.

"Govinda, why did You let this happen? Why did You let me love a man who never loved me?"

Silence.

The same silence that filled her house. The same silence that had replaced Arjun's laughter.

The Final Betrayal

Weeks later, she had found out the final betrayal—Arjun was already married. To someone else.

A temple wedding. Grand. Lavish. He had married another woman in the presence of the same God she had once begged for their love to last.

That night, Suneetha had wanted to end it all. What was left for her in this world? A life filled with emptiness? A bed that was too big for one? A heart that could never be whole again?

The Strabger by the Steps

Yet, something—some unseen force—kept her from taking that final step.

And so, she found herself at Tirumala once more, her tears falling onto the cold stone steps.She looked up at the sanctum, her voice breaking as she whispered, "Govinda, why? Why did You let me live when You took everything away?"

The wind howled through the temple corridors, but no divine voice answered. No miracle unfolded.Only a bitter realization settled in her heart—not every wound heals. Not every heartbreak finds closure.

Some wounds remain open. Some love stories don't end with new beginnings.

And sometimes, even Govinda is silent.

Suneetha wiped her tears, her chest aching as she turned away from the temple.

She had come seeking comfort, but she was leaving just as broken as she had arrived.

As she descended the steps, her vision blurred with unshed tears, she barely noticed an old man sitting nearby, feeding a few stray dogs. His frail hands trembled slightly as he tore a piece of roti and placed it before them. There was something about him—his stillness, his quiet wisdom—that made her pause.

Sensing her presence, he glanced up and smiled. "Why do you cry, child?"

Suneetha swallowed the lump in her throat. "I have lost everything," she whispered.

The old man nodded knowingly, as if he had heard these words a thousand times before. "No, my dear. You have only lost what was never truly yours."

His words made her heart ache even more. "Then why does it hurt so much?"

The old man placed a hand over his heart. "Because love, when placed in the wrong hands, always leads to pain. When we hold on to something that isn't meant for us, Govinda removes it—painfully, but for a reason. He doesn't take away love, child. He only redirects it."

Suneetha clenched her fists. "Then why didn't He save my marriage? Why didn't He stop me from loving a man who never loved me?"

Govinda Stands with Me

The old man smiled sadly. "Because Govinda does not force anyone to stay in our lives. If someone chooses to leave, it is not your loss. It is theirs. You begged for Arjun, but Govinda was protecting you from him. You prayed for love, but He is preparing you for something greater. Sometimes, unanswered prayers are His greatest mercy."

Suneetha felt something shift inside her.

Had she been mourning a love that was never meant to last? Had she been blind to the protection she had mistaken for punishment?

A sudden gust of wind swept through the temple corridors, carrying the distant chants of "Govinda... Govinda..."into the air. For the first time, those words didn't feel distant. They didn't feel like a cry into emptiness.

They felt like a reminder.

She had lost love. She had lost dreams. But she had not lost herself.

And as she walked down the temple steps, alone yet unbroken, she knew—Govinda still stood with her.

Even in the silence.

Even in the heartbreak.

Even in the loneliness.

And that was enough

VII
Faith Never Fails

Devotee is From Tirupathi

Srivatsav, a simple and innocent village boy, joined a prestigious multinational company, bringing with him unwavering faith in Govinda. His devotion, humility, and traditional ways made him stand out in the fast-paced corporate world. But instead of admiration, he became a target of mockery.

"Does Govinda help you finish reports too?" his colleagues sneered.

"Maybe he'll show up in the meeting and do your work!" another laughed.

Srivatsav never reacted. He simply smiled and said, *"Govinda sees everything."*

But one man despised him the most—his manager, Rahul.

Rahul's Hatred for Devotion

Rahul had no interest in faith or devotion. He saw them as signs of weakness and loved to mock those who believed in bhakti. He considered spirituality useless in the corporate world, where he believed power and politics ruled.Seeing Srivatsav's calmness, his honesty, and his quiet way of working irritated Rahul.

"Why doesn't this fool try to impress anyone? Why isn't he afraid?"

It angered him even more that, despite being laughed at, Srivatsav never reacted.

"People like him don't belong here," Rahul thought. *"I'll teach him a lesson he won't forget."*

The Ultimate Humiliation

A crucial client presentation was scheduled, and Rahul saw his opportunity. He assigned Srivatsav the responsibility, pretending to trust him. But just before the meeting, he secretly deleted all of Srivatsav's files.

As Srivatsav connected his laptop, the screen flickered—his entire presentation was gone.

Rahul smirked. *"Oh no! Maybe Govinda took your work with Him!"*

The entire room erupted in laughter.

The CEO, unimpressed, warned, *"You have five minutes. If you can't present, you're out."*

Srivatsav's hands trembled. His heart pounded. He had never felt so humiliated.

"Govinda... why?" he whispered.

The Divine Twist

Just then, a notification popped up—"Auto-recovery successful."

His entire presentation reappeared, intact.

Gasps filled the room. The IT team, confused, checked the system logs.

"This... this isn't possible. The files were deleted from the main server," one of them shocked.

Ignoring the shock around him, Srivatsav took a deep breath and whispered, *"Govinda."* Then, with calm confidence, he delivered the presentation flawlessly.

The CEO was highly impressed. *"Brilliant work, Srivatsav. This is exactly what we needed!"*

Silence filled the room. The same people who had laughed at him minutes ago were now speechless.

The Truth Comes Out

The IT team investigated the file loss and uncovered the shocking truth—Rahul had deliberately deleted the files.

The CEO's face darkened. *"You tried to harm your own employee? You're fired."*

Rahul stood frozen, his confidence shattered. Everything he had done to humiliate Srivatsav had backfired.

He turned to Srivatsav, his voice shaking. *"How did your files come back?"*

Srivatsav simply smiled. *"Govinda takes care of everything."*

The Silent Realization

No one spoke. No one laughed.

They had mocked him, humilated his devotion, and watched him suffer—but in the end, something beyond logic had saved him.

One by one, they lowered their heads, realizing the truth.

Never look down on people who have faith. If mocking them feels fun at the moment, remember—one day, it may come back to you. Govinda is always beside those who trust Him. When the time comes, He will definitely teach you.

VIII

A Second Chance: From Struggle to Strength

<u>*Devotee is From Visakhapatnam*</u>

Vikram was 27. Jobless. Humiliated. Used by friends. Insulted by relatives. His parents were ashamed of him. Society had only one name for him—"useless."

One day, he saw a job opening, a golden chance to turn his life around. But fate played its cruel game again—he needed ₹100 for the application fee. He searched everywhere. No one gave him a single rupee. His so-called friends laughed. His relatives mocked, "You'll never earn even ₹10 in your life!" His father scolded him, his mother turned away.

Desperate, one night, he stole ₹100 from the almirah.

But he got caught. His uncle saw him.

"THIEF!" The word struck like thunder.

By morning, the entire family knew. Neighbors gathered, whispering and sneering. His father's face burned with shame. His mother's eyes filled with silent disappointment. Even street vendors gossiped, "So that's what he has become?" His name was ruined forever.

That night, unable to bear it, he disappeared. He left home, left the town—without telling anyone where he was going.

A New Path Begins...

Days later, he arrived at Tirumala. Alone. Lost. He had no food, no money, nowhere to go. He wandered near the temple, watching devotees come with prayers and return with hope. But what prayer could a thief like him offer?

For days, he survived by sleeping outside, eating what little prasadam was given to him. He saw devotees walking barefoot, shedding their burdens before the Lord. He saw men who had lost everything still bowing before Govinda, with faith stronger than gold.

One night, exhausted, he collapsed near the temple steps. An old man, dressed like a pilgrim, sat beside him and said, "Son, why do you run? The world has already punished you. Will you punish yourself too?"

Vikram broke down. "They called me a thief... Maybe I am."

The old man smiled, "Do you know what people called Balaji when He stood silent, letting His devotees suffer their karma? They called Him heartless. Did it change who He was?"

Vikram stared.

"Son, the world will throw dirt at you. You decide whether to carry it or wash it away."

That night, something changed. He realized he was not a thief. He was a man who had let the world define him.

Rising from the Ashes

The next morning, he took a deep breath and walked toward the temple. He stood before Sri Venkateswara Swamy and whispered, "I will not beg for mercy. I will prove myself."

From that day, he worked. He started as a helper in a small eatery, carrying plates, cleaning floors. Then, he became a temple volunteer, helping devotees, washing their feet, serving prasadam. Slowly, his pain turned into strength. His past faded. People no longer whispered, "Thief." They now called him "the man who never gave up."

Years passed. He didn't return home. He built a new life, far from the shadows of his past. From a worker, he became a chef. From a chef, a manager. Then, one day, he opened his own hotel.

He named it "Govinda Bhavan."

It wasn't just a hotel—it was a symbol.

Every Saturday, free meals were served to the poor.

For every job seeker, the first ₹100 of their journey was given—because he knew how it felt to need it.

One evening, as he stood watching people eat, an old man entered, his hands trembling. His father.

Vikram didn't move. His father did. He stepped forward, placed ₹100 on the counter, and with tears in his eyes, said, "I don't know if I came to eat or to return what I never gave you."

Vikram smiled softly and pushed the money back. "Keep it. I never needed it. I only needed a chance."

The boy they once called a thief had become a man who gave hope.

IX

The Last Hope

Devotee is From HyderabadVikram was a successful businessman in Hyderabad, but despite his wealth, his life felt empty. His only son, Aditya, had been diagnosed with a rare heart condition, and doctors had given up hope. "A transplant is the only option," they said, "but finding a donor in time is nearly impossible."

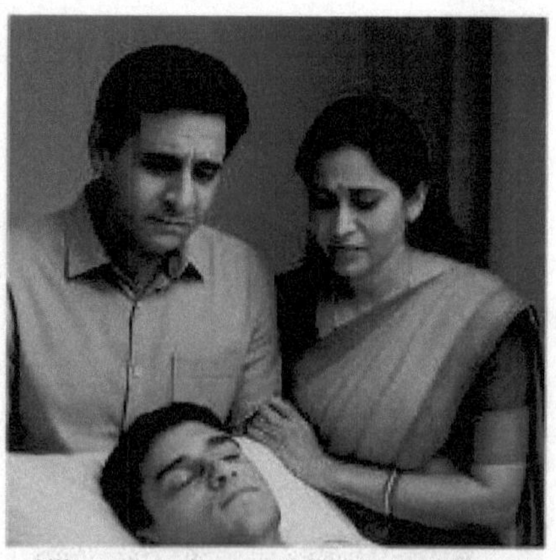

Vikram's only son, Aditya, needed
a heart transplant

Vikram, who had never been deeply religious, found himself drawn to Lord Venkateswara. His wife, Ananya, insisted they go to Tirumala and pray. "Only He can save our son," she pleaded. Desperate, Vikram agreed.

Reaching Tirumala, Vikram stood before the deity, tears in his eyes. "Swamy, I have always relied on my own strength, but today, I surrender to You. If my son survives, I will dedicate my life to serving You." He made an offering and returned with a heavy heart.

Days passed, and Aditya's condition worsened. One evening, the hospital received an unexpected call—there was a donor, a young man who had met with an accident, and his family had agreed to donate his heart. The transplant was scheduled immediately.

The surgery was a success, but what left everyone speechless was the donor's identity. He was a devotee returning from Tirumala, and in his wallet was a small note: "If anything happens to me, let my life serve someone in need. Govinda Govinda!"

A donor was found, and Aditya received a new heart

Vikram and Ananya wept before the Lord. Aditya had been given a second life, not just through the donor but through divine intervention. From that day, Vikram kept his promise—he built free medical camps near Tirumala, serving countless devotees, his heart forever devoted to the Lord who had saved his son.

X
Overcoming Fear and Finding Hope

<u>*Devotee is From Vijayawada*</u>

Sindhu was a hardworking girl, but she was always scared—especially about her IIT JEE Main results. She had already lost one year trying to get a seat in IIT. Even though she worked hard, fear never left her mind.

Her parents were very strict and didn't want her to take coaching again. But she convinced them and put in all her efforts. She got a good score in the prelims, but the mains paper was very tough. Since the exam, she had been living in fear, unable to sleep properly at night.

The results day finally arrived. As she had feared, her score was not good. She didn't know how to tell her parents. Even though she had studied so hard, she couldn't achieve what she wanted. The fear and disappointment crushed her.

She was scared to tell her parents. Her mind was filled with negative thoughts. She started thinking, Why should I live? No one understands me. She sat in a corner, crying.

At that moment, she remembered something her grandmother had told her. "Whenever you feel hopeless, read the Sri Venkateswara Swamy Vajra Kavacha Stotram. Swamy will protect you."

She had always kept a small picture of Sri Venkateswara Swamy in her pocket, given by her grandmother. Though she had never read the stotram before, that day, with tears in her eyes, she read it.

Even after reading it, her pain didn't go away immediately. She went home and told her parents about the results. As expected, they were angry and scolded her. Unable to bear it, she ran out of the house.

The Miracle

Without realizing where she was going, she kept walking and suddenly found herself in front of a small Sri Venkateswara Swamy temple. She was crying, feeling completely lost. But then, she remembered her grandmother's words again.

Inside the temple, a priest was chanting the Vishnu Sahasranamam. The divine atmosphere gave her some peace. She walked forward, held the Swamy's photo in her hands, and prayed sincerely:

"Swamy, I have worked so hard. But why did I fail? I don't know what to do. Please help me. I don't want to feel this fear anymore."

At that moment, something unexpected happened. A gentle breeze blew inside the temple. The priest, who was about to leave, suddenly turned toward Sindhu and smiled.

He said, "Child, don't lose hope. Sometimes, what we want doesn't come to us immediately. That doesn't mean we are not worthy. Swamy has bigger plans for you. Surrender your fear to him."

Hearing those words, Sindhu felt something change inside her. It was as if a heavy burden had been lifted. She realized that one failure didn't mean the end of everything.

With a calm mind, she returned home. She apologized to her parents and decided to try again—but this time, without fear. She continued her studies with complete faith in Sri Venkateswara Swamy.

A year later, she wrote the exam again—and this time, she cleared it!

She knew it was only because of Swamy's blessings that she had overcome her fear and achieved success. From that day onward, she believed that whenever life gets tough, faith and effort together bring miracles.

XI
Sri Srinivasa Kalyanam

1. The Yajna of the Sages

At the start of Kaliyuga, a group of great sages were performing a yajna on the banks of the sacred River Ganga for the well-being of the world. At that moment, the celestial sage Narada appeared and asked them, "To whom will you offer the fruits of this yajna?" The sages could not agree on an answer.

Narada advised them to test the three supreme deities—Brahma, Vishnu, and Shiva—and give the merit of the yajna to the most deserving. Sage Bhrigu, one of the great sages, was chosen for this task

2. The Test of the Trimurtis

Bhrigu Visits Lord Brahma: Sage Bhrigu first went to Satyaloka, the divine abode of Lord Brahma. There, he saw Lord Brahma reciting the four Vedas in praise of Lord Narayana with His four heads, while Goddess Saraswati attended to Him.

However, Lord Brahma did not notice Sage Bhrigu offering his respects. Feeling disrespected, Bhrigu concluded that Brahma was not worthy of worship and left for Kailasa, the sacred abode of Lord Shiva.

Bhrigu Visits Lord Shiva: At Kailasa, Bhrigu found Lord Shiva sitting with Goddess Parvati, yet once again, Shiva did not notice his presence. When Parvati pointed this out, Shiva became angry and tried to destroy the sage. Hurt by this, Bhrigu cursed Lord Shiva and left for Vaikuntam

Bhrigu Visits Lord Vishnu: At Vaikuntam, Lord Vishnu (Srimannarayana) was resting peacefully on Adisesha, with Goddess Lakshmi serving at His feet. When Bhrigu arrived, Lord Vishnu did not acknowledge him either. In his anger, Bhrigu kicked Lord Vishnu on the chest, the very place where Goddess Lakshmi resides

Then, Lord Vishnu, creator & protector of this universe, massaged the feet of Brigu and closed the 3rd eye which is under the feet of Brigu. Then, Brigu understood his mistake and asked to forgive him. He went to all the sages and said that only Vishnu can be offered the yagnaphalam.

Lord Vishnu didn't punished or cursed Bhrigu (sage) even if he kicked on his chest. Further, he massaged the feet of Bhrigu! Through this, he's telling us to be patient (patience is too important. This doesn't mean that be patient even if your Dharma is disgraced by others.) Mainly, the people who want to be a devotee and protect our dharma should have patience to fulfill their wish.

3. The Departure of Goddess Lakshmi

Lakshmi Devi was heartbroken that someone had kicked her Lord on His chest, her own home, and that Vishnu did not react. Filled with sorrow, she left Vaikuntha and came down to Earth. This marked the beginning of a divine story.

4. Lord Srinivasa on Earth

In his search for his beloved consort Lakshmi Devi, Sri Vishnu departed from Vaikuntam and arrived at Venkatachalam. During his time there, he experienced the hardship of thirst and hunger, just like an ordinary human being. In fact, he even resided in an anthill under a tamarind tree, beside a pushkarini on the Venkata Hill.. Learning about Vishnu's situation from Surya deva, Lakshmi, his consort, became very sorrowful. Consequently, she travelled to the place where Vishnu was staying and sold a cow and calf to the Chola's queen.

Interestingly, Lord Shiva and Lord Brahma took on the form of the cow and calf. Because of her deep faith in them, Lakshmi sold the cow and calf to the queen, and then moved on to Kolhapur.

5. The Divine Cow Episode

Each day, the cow and calf secretly gave milk to Srinivasa. The queen, seeing her cow not yielding milk, blamed her servant and punished him. Then, the next day, that servant followed the cow and calf and saw the cow giving milk to Srinivasa. With so much of angry, he threw the axe on the cow.

To protect cow, Srinivasa came out of the anthill. That axe hit Srinivasa on the forehead and made Him bleed. When the cowherd saw that Swamy was hurt and bleeding because of his axe, he was so shocked that he fell to the ground and died.The cow got scared and ran back to the Chola King, crying and covered in blood.

The King wanted to know what had happened, so he followed the cow. When he reached the place, he saw the cowherd lying dead near an ant-hill. While the King was standing there confused, Swamy came out from the ant-hill and cursed the King. He said the King would become a demon (Asura) because of the mistake made by his servant.The King said he was innocent and didn't know about it. Then Swamy told him that the curse would end in the future when Swamy wore a crown (kireetam) given by Akasa Raja during His marriage with Sri Padmavati.

6. Lord Srinivasa Meets Varaha Swamy and Vakula Devi

After that, Lord Srinivasa called Brihaspathi and asked for a medicine to cure his pain. As advised by Brihaspathi, Swamy went in search of the medicine and met Varaha swamy and asked a place to live.

Srinivasa said to Varaha swamy "I don't have money now as Lakshmi left me. But, I'll give promises that I'll become a deity here and daily offer you Milk. After your naivedyam only, I'll eat and also devotees must first have your darsan in Tirumala yatra before they come to my temple. Varaha swamy agreed for that and said to reside in the asramam of Vakuladevi (Yasoda in her previous life). She cured the pain of Srinivasa by giving medicines and thought him as her child.

Yashoda brought up Sri Krishna, the son of Devaki, during His early years. But she was not blessed to witness His marriage with Rukmini and felt very sad. Sri Krishna consoled her and promised that in her next birth as Vakuladevi, she would witness His marriage when He appears again as Srinivasa. In her next life, Yashoda was born as Vakuladevi and was serving Lord Varahaswami. Later, Varahaswami sent her to lovingly serve Srinivasa.

7. The Birth of Padmavati Devi

Around the same time, a king named Akasa Raja from the sacred Lunar race was ruling Thondamandalam. He had a brother named Thondaman. Since the king had no children, he decided to perform a holy sacrifice. While preparing land for a yajna, he found a lotus with a divine baby girl inside. Filled with joy, he took the child to his palace and gave her to his queen. Just then, a heavenly voice said, "O

King, raise her as your daughter. Great fortune will come to you." As she was found in a lotus, he named her Padmavati. Later, his wife Dharani Devi gave birth to a son named Vasudan.

8. Lord Srinivasa and Padmavati Devi's First Meeting

Padmavati and Vasudan grew up. One day, Padmavati went to the garden with her friends. There, Sage Narada appeared. He told her that he was her well-wisher and asked to see her palm to read her future. After looking at it, he said that she was destined to marry none other than Lord Vishnu Himself. At this time, Lord Srinivasa, who was hunting, chased a wild elephant in the forests surrounding the hills. In the elephant's pursuit, the Lord was led into a garden, where Princess Padmavati and her maids were picking flowers, and asked about Padmavati. When he proposed, Padmavati didn't say anything to Srinivasa, and her friends threw stones at him due to misunderstanding, later Srinivasa returned to Ashram.

9. Marriage Proposal and Soothsayer's Visit

VakulaMata noticed blood on Srinivasa's body, applied butter, and inquired about what happened. Srinivasa explained everything, asking Vakula to approach the king regarding Padmavati's marriage. He shared Padmavati's previous birth story (Vedavati). Vakula agreed, went to the city, and worshipped Lord Shiva at Agasthyeswara temple. Padmavati's friends, worried about her, also visited the temple for Rudrabhishekam. Vakula met them, seeking guidance on meeting Queen Dharani Devi. Introducing herself as a servant of Srinivasa swamy, she expressed her purpose. The friends, identified as Padmavati's sakhis, agreed and provided an introduction.

There, Srinivasa thought to help his mother, Vakula, in arranging marriage and went as an old soothsayer nearby the palace of Aakasa Raju. Servants of the queen saw her and invited her to the palace on the order of Dharani Devi. The soothsayer spoke about the meeting of Padmavati and Srinivasa in the garden. She also revealed that Srinivasa is none other than Srimannarayana. Dharani Devi didn't believe her words.

Then, the soothsayer said, "If you want proof, see, a lady sent by Srinivasa comes with a marriage proposal." After telling this, she went off. Dharani Devi was surprised and went to Padmavati Maa. She asked Padmavati why she was sad. Then, Padmavati spoke about meeting Srinivasa Swamy and also mentioned that he is Srimannarayana himself and not an ordinary man. After this, Vakula devi, with the friends of Padmavati, went to Dharani Devi with a marriage proposal. Dharani Devi agreed.

10. *Fixing the Wedding Date*

After approval of the marriage from the all ends, King Akasaraja wanted to fix an auspicious date. He invited Brihaspati, the guru of the gods, for this important task. The king suggested that since Padmavati's birth star was Margashirsha and Lord Srinivasa's was Shravana, the wedding should take place when these stars align. After careful thought, Brihaspati chose the Uttaraphalguni day in the month of Vaisakha as the best time. Pleased with this decision, Akasaraja honored Brihaspati and sent him off with respect.

11. *Message Sent to Lord Srinivasa*

To inform Lord Srinivasa about the wedding date, Akasaraja sent Suka, a trusted messenger of Queen Dharani. Suka, accompanied by Bakulamalika, rode on horseback to Venkatadri. Upon reaching, Suka conveyed the message of Padmavati's deep devotion. She expressed how she always chants His name, wears His symbols, serves His devotees, and follows rituals that please Him.

12. Lord Srinivasa's Gift to Padmavati

Hearing Padmavati's words, Lord Srinivasa was touched. As a token of His love, He gave Suka a garland made of basil and scented with musk to be presented to Padmavati. Suka returned to Narayanapura and gave the garland to Padmavati. Filled with joy, she humbly bowed her head and placed the garland on herself. She eagerly awaited the arrival of the Lord on the wedding day

However, before proceeding, Lord Srinivasa felt it was necessary to speak with Ramadevi (Goddess Lakshmi), residing within him. He invited her and, with utmost reverence, shared his intention to marry Padmavathi.

Ramadevi, embodying boundless wisdom and grace, smiled gently. "How can I say no? You know what to do and when to do it. After all, this is not just a wedding—it is the fulfillment of a promise. A promise made to Vedavathi, whose devotion has endured through time."

13. Ramadevi and the Fulfillment of Vedavati's Promise

At that moment, the celestial realms seemed to resonate with the echoes of an ancient vow. The story of Vedavathi, a woman of unparalleled devotion, unfolded in Srinivasa's mind.

Long ago, in the Treta Yuga, Vedavathi was a devoted ascetic who worshipped Lord Vishnu, desiring only to be his consort. When Ravana, the king of Lanka, attempted to dishonor her, she sacrificed herself in a pyre, vowing that she would return to be the cause of his downfall. True to her word, she was reborn as Sita, the divine wife of Lord Rama (Vishnu's avatar).

Yet, destiny had another test for her. When Lord Rama questioned Sita's purity after the war, she entered the Agni Pariksha (trial by fire). But what emerged from the flames was not just Sita—Vedavathi was released from her role, free to continue her divine journey.

With unwavering devotion, Vedavathi sought another birth where she could truly be with Vishnu as his consort. And so, she was reborn as Padmavathi, the princess of the Pallava dynasty, fulfilling the divine plan.

As Lord Srinivasa stood in deep contemplation, Ramadevi's voice brought him back to the present.

"You promised Vedavathi that you would accept her. This marriage is not just a union—it is the fulfillment of a sacred bond that spans ages."

Srinivasa nodded. This wedding was not only the culmination of Padmavathi's fate but the completion of Vedavathi's devotion. The heavens rejoiced, and the universe prepared to witness the long-awaited reunion of Lord Vishnu and his eternal devotee.

And so, with divine blessings, the wedding of Lord Srinivasa and Goddess Padmavathi was celebrated with unmatched grandeur, marking the fulfillment of a promise made in the flames of devotion and realized in the celestial bonds of love.

14. Preparations for the Grand Wedding

Akasaraja wanted the wedding to be perfect, so he called upon the gods for assistance. He sent his son Vasudana to invite Indra and other celestial beings. The gods happily took part in the preparations:

- Vishwakarma decorated the city beautifully.
- Indra showered flowers from the sky.
- Celestial maidens performed graceful dances.
- Kubera ensured an abundance of wealth and food.
- Yama granted people good health and freed them from illness.
- Varuna filled the land with sparkling jewels and precious stones.
- Chandra (the Moon God) used his nectarine rays to prepare food worthy of the Lord.

Once everything was ready, the gods proceeded to Vrishachala to join the bridegroom's party. On the wedding day, Queen Dharani adorned her daughter with exquisite ornaments and waited for the grand procession.

15. Lord Srinivasa's Wedding Procession

On the special day, Lakshmi Devi and other celestial attendants adorned Lord Srinivasa with great care:

- Priti (Pleasure) brought fragrant oils.
- Sruti (Vedas) provided silk garments.
- Smriti (Code of Conduct) offered precious ornaments.
- Dhriti (Fortitude) handed Him a mirror.
- Shanti (Peace) brought musk.
- Siri (Prosperity) gave a divine perfume.
- Kirti (Fame) presented a golden crown studded with gems.
- Indrani held the royal umbrella.
- Saraswati and Gauri waved fans.
- Jaya and Vijaya held fly whisks.

Lakshmi Devi carefully applied scented oil to the Lord and bathed Him with water from celestial rivers, stored in golden pots carried by divine elephants. She tied His hair, dressed Him in blue silk, and adorned Him with waistbands, rings, and other ornaments. Finally, Lord Srinivasa looked into the mirror and applied the sacred Urdhvapundra mark on His forehead.

Lord Srinivasa, along with Lakshmi Devi mounted Garuda and set off for Narayanapura. Brahma, Shiva, Varuna, Yama, Kubera, Vasishtha, Sanaka, and many great sages accompanied them. Celestial musicians played divine instruments, Gandharvas sang melodious tunes, and heavenly maidens danced in joy. The entire sky was filled with the sound of drums and Vedic chants. Vishwaksena, Bakulamalika, and other celestial beings followed in chariots, making the procession truly grand.

16. Devi Padmavati's Royal Welcome

King Akasaraja, seeing the splendid arrival of the Lord, made special arrangements to welcome Him. Devi Padmavati was seated on the celestial elephant Airavata and taken on a procession around the city. The entire kingdom rejoiced as they witnessed the divine bride and groom coming together.

17. The Exchange of Garlands

At the beautifully decorated gateway, Lord Srinivasa and Devi Padmavati met. They sat on their respective divine vehicles and exchanged garlands as a sign of their sacred bond. Lord Srinivasa lovingly placed a garland from His neck onto Padmavati, and she, in turn, offered Him a fragrant jasmine garland. They repeated this ritual three times before stepping down from their vehicles.

18. The Sacred Wedding Ceremony

Lord Srinivasa and Padmavathi Devi entered the grand marriage hall, where Lord Brahma himself performed the sacred rituals. He began by tying the Mangalasutra (sacred thread) and concluded with Laja Homa (offering grains into the fire for prosperity). The rituals continued for four days, filling the air with divine energy and devotion. Once the ceremony was complete, the gods and celestial beings took leave of Akasaraja, showering their blessings on the newly married couple.

Thus, the divine wedding of Lord Srinivasa and Devi Padmavati took place with immense joy and grandeur, marking the union of two divine souls for the welfare of the world

In Devotion To Govinda

Author's Note

I have shared the native places of the devotees to help you connect with where their journeys began. Their personal identities have been kept private out of respect for their wishes and to protect their privacy.

These are not just stories — they are real experiences shared with deep emotion and trust. I truly believe in them because they reflect the kind of faith, struggles, and miracles that many devotees of Govinda go through. Each one holds a piece of truth, pain, and divine grace.

Thank you for reading with an open heart.

www.ingramcontent.com/pod-product-compliance
Lightning Source LLC
Chambersburg PA
CBHW031458150726
47990CB00007B/2802